EASIEST
BOOK *of*
PIANO
CLASSICS

Amsco Publications
New York/London/Sydney

Order No. AM 942095
US International Standard Book Number: 0.8256.1596.8
UK International Standard Book Number: 0.7119.6287.1

Exclusive Distributors:
Music Sales Corporation
257 Park Avenue South, New York, NY 10010 USA
Music Sales Limited
8/9 Frith Street, London W1V 5TZ England
Music Sales Pty. Limited
120 Rothschild Street, Rosebery, Sydney, NSW 2018, Australia

Printed in the United States of America by
Vicks Lithograph and Printing Corporation

Contents

Studio

Johann Christoph Friedrich Bach

Allegretto Scherzando

Carl Philipp Emanuel Bach

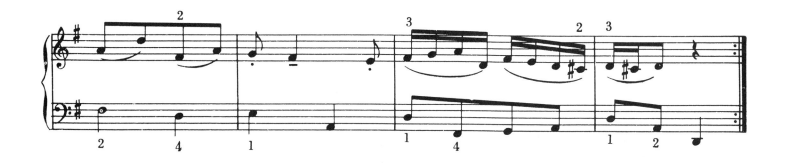

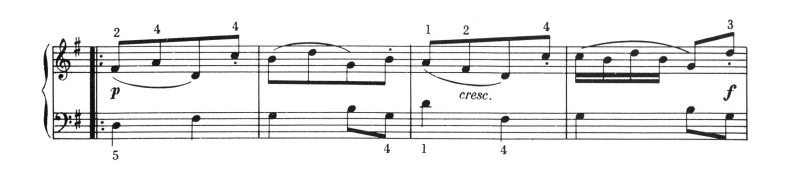

Prelude in C from 12 Little Preludes

Johann Sebastian Bach

Air on the G String

Johann Sebastian Bach

Jesu, Joy of Man's Desiring

Johann Sebastian Bach

March from Anna Magdalena's Notebook

Johann Sebastian Bach

Minuet from Anna Magdalena's Notebook

Johann Sebastian Bach

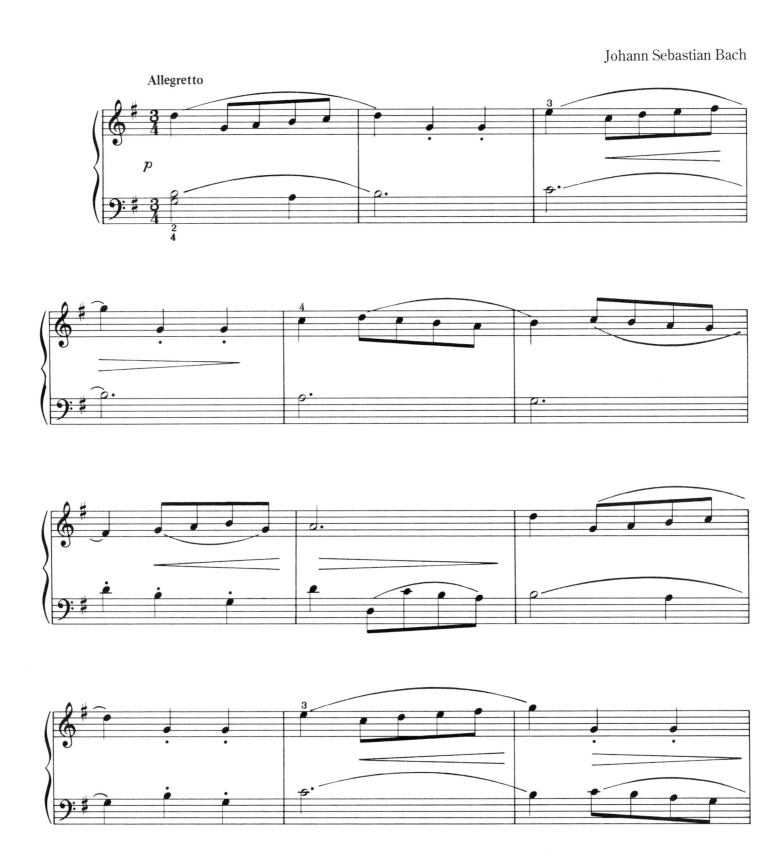

Minuet from French Suite No. 6

Johann Sebastian Bach

Minuet from Partita No. 1

Johann Sebastian Bach

Musette from Anna Magdalena's Notebook

Johann Sebastian Bach

Polonaise

Johann Sebastian Bach

Sarabande

Johann Sebastian Bach

Sheep May Safely Graze

Johann Sebastian Bach

Wachet auf

Johann Sebastian Bach

Air

Wilhelm Friedemann Bach

Moderato

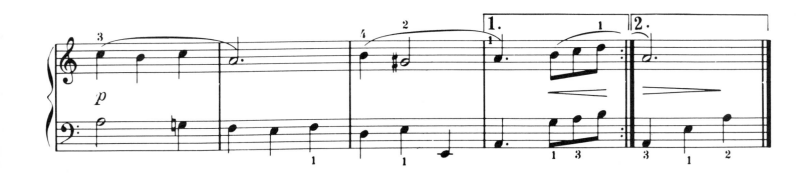

Adagio from Pathétique Sonata

Ludwig van Beethoven

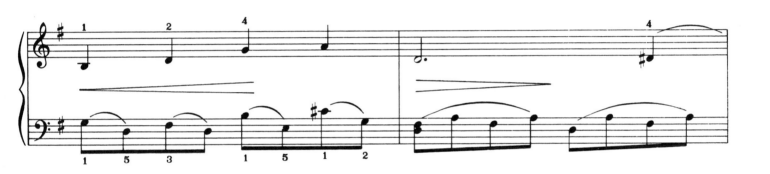

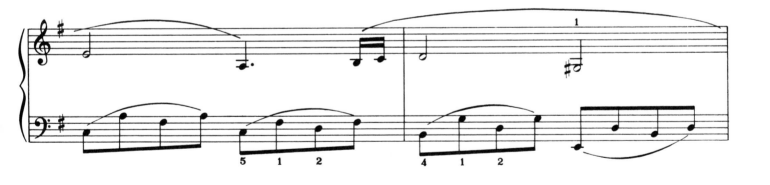

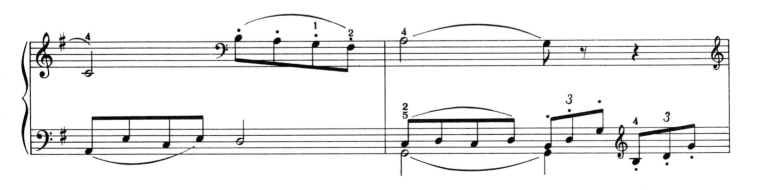

36

Allegretto from Sonata Op. 14, No. 1

Ludwig van Beethoven

Bagatelle Op. 33, No. 6

Ludwig van Beethoven

Moderato

Emperor Concerto First Movement

Ludwig van Beethoven

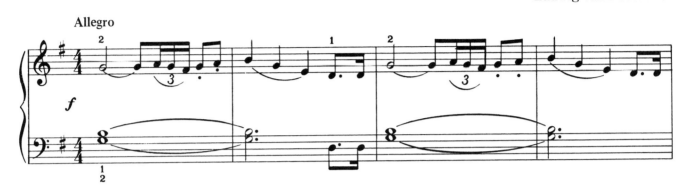

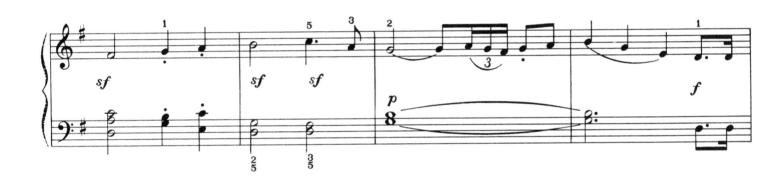

Für Elise

Ludwig van Beethoven

Eroica Symphony (Theme)

Ludwig van Beethoven

47

March from Egmont Overture

Ludwig van Beethoven

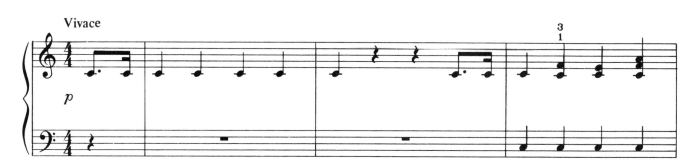

Minuet in G

Ludwig van Beethoven

Moonlight Sonata First Movement

Ludwig van Beethoven

52

Symphony No. 9 Theme from Finale

Ludwig van Beethoven

Violin Concerto (First Movement)

Ludwig van Beethoven

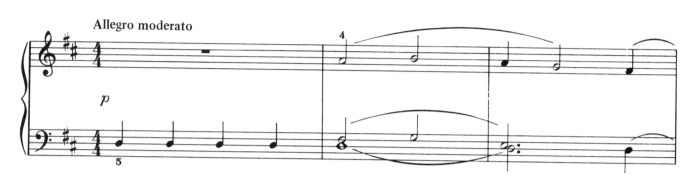

In May

Franz Behr

The Flower Song
from Carmen

Georges Bizet

62

Habanera
from Carmen

Georges Bizet

Toreador's Song
from Carmen

Georges Bizet

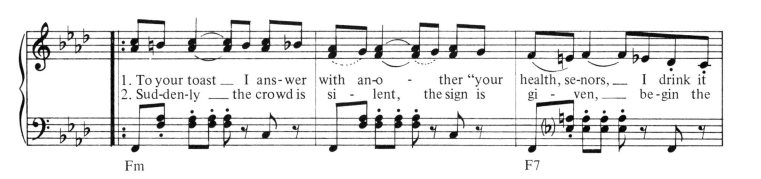

1. To your toast __ I ans-wer with an-o - ther "your health, se-nors, __ I drink it
2. Sud-den-ly __ the crowd is si - lent, the sign is gi - ven, __ be-gin the

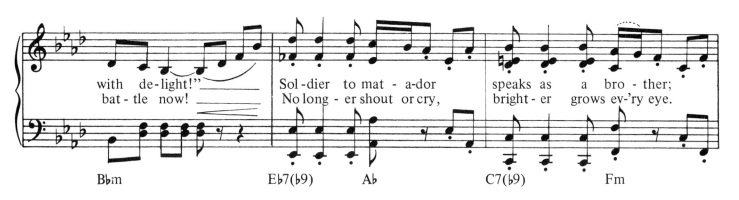

with de-light!" __ Sol-dier to mat - a-dor speaks as a bro - ther;
bat - tle now! __ No long - er shout or cry, bright - er grows ev-'ry eye.

70

Polovtsian Dances

Alexander Borodin

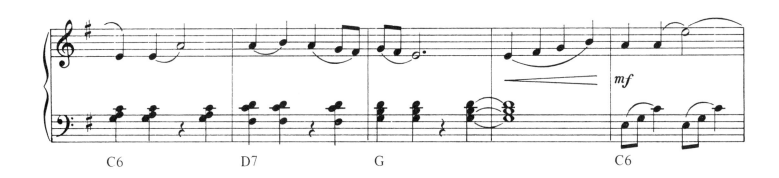

Hungarian Dance No. 6

Johannes Brahms

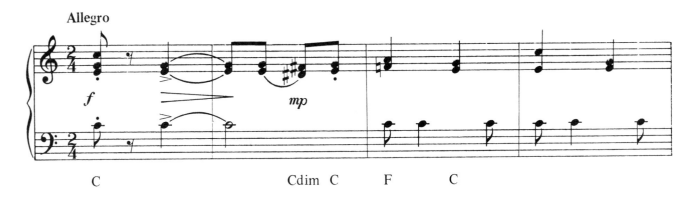

Theme
from 4th Movement Symphony No. 1

Johannes Brahms

Berceuse

Frédéric Chopin

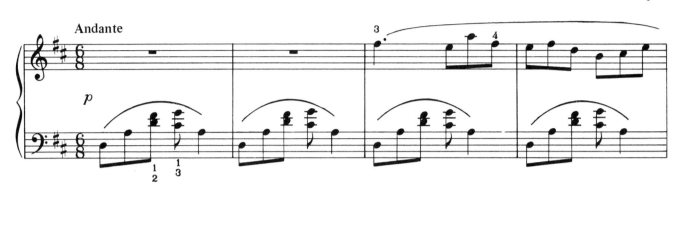

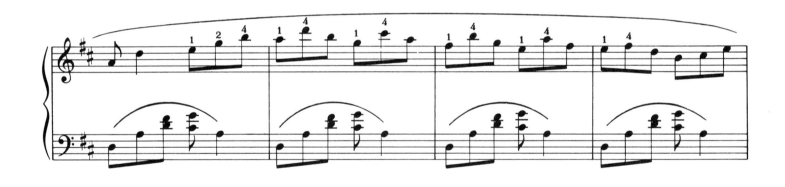

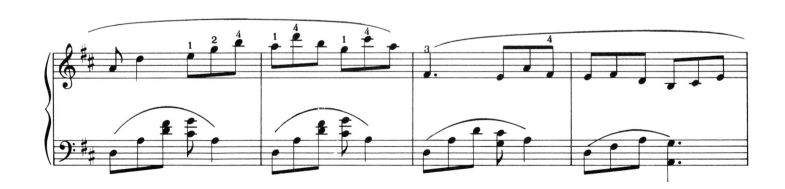

Etude No. 3

Frédéric Chopin

Funeral March from Sonata Op. 35, No. 2

Frédéric Chopin

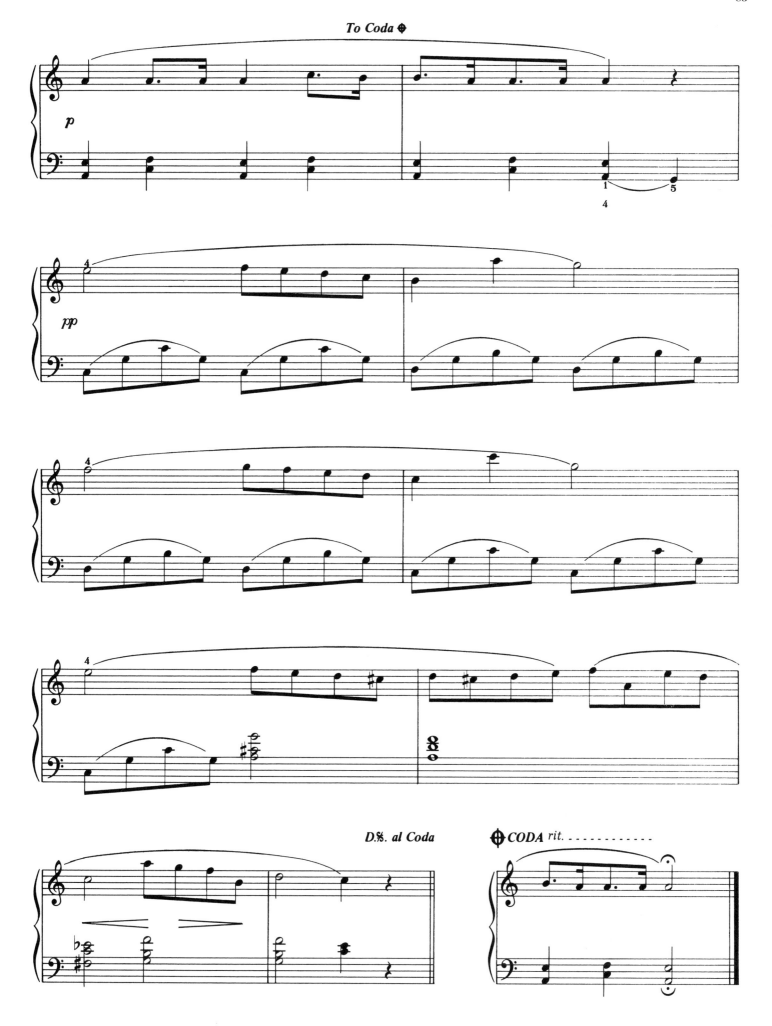

Mazurka Op. 7, No. 1

Frédéric Chopin

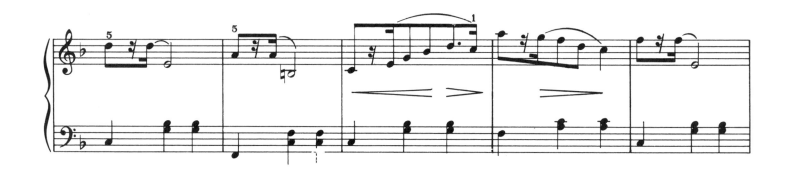

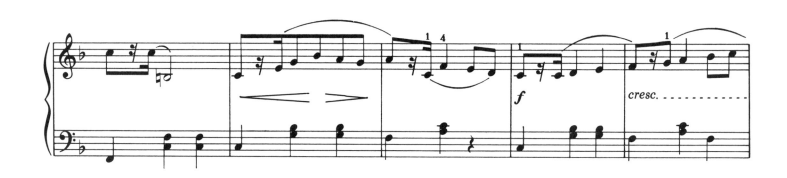

Nocturne Op. 55, No. 1

Frédéric Chopin

Theme from Ballade Op. 23

Frédéric Chopin

Moderato

Polonaise Op. 40, No. 1

Frédéric Chopin

D.C. al Fine

Prelude (Raindrop) Op. 28, No. 15

Frédéric Chopin

Theme from Fantaisie Impromptu Op. 66

Frédéric Chopin

Theme from Sonata Op. 58

Frédéric Chopin

Waltz Op. 64, No. 2

Frédéric Chopin

Clair de lune

Claude Debussy

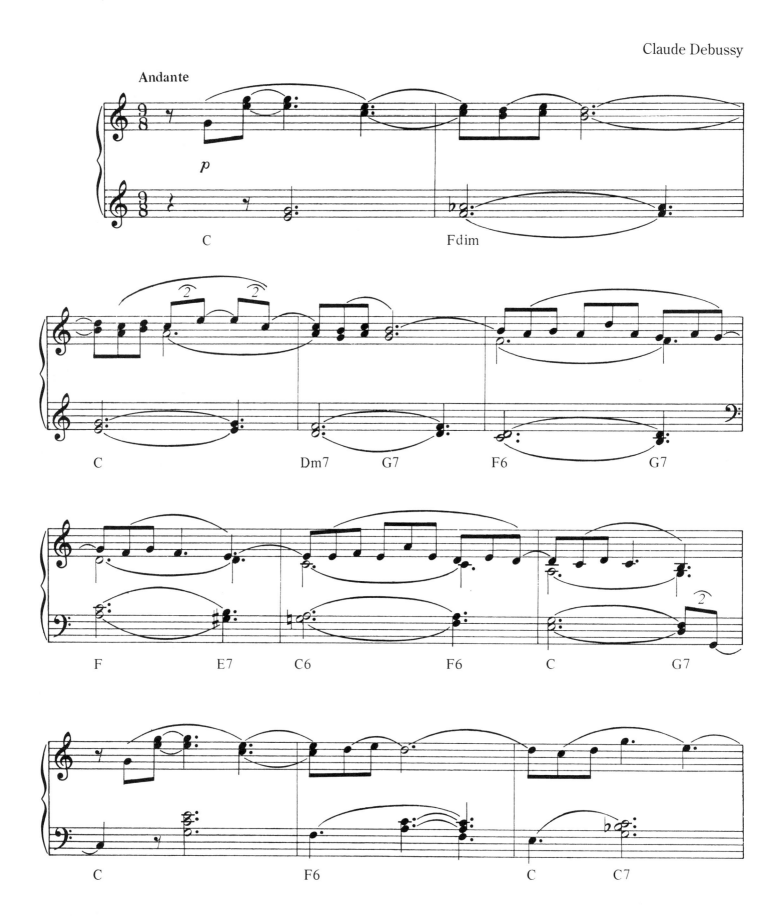

Waltz
from Coppélia

Léo Delibes

103

Pizzicati
from Sylvia

Léo Delibes

Walking

Anton Diabelli

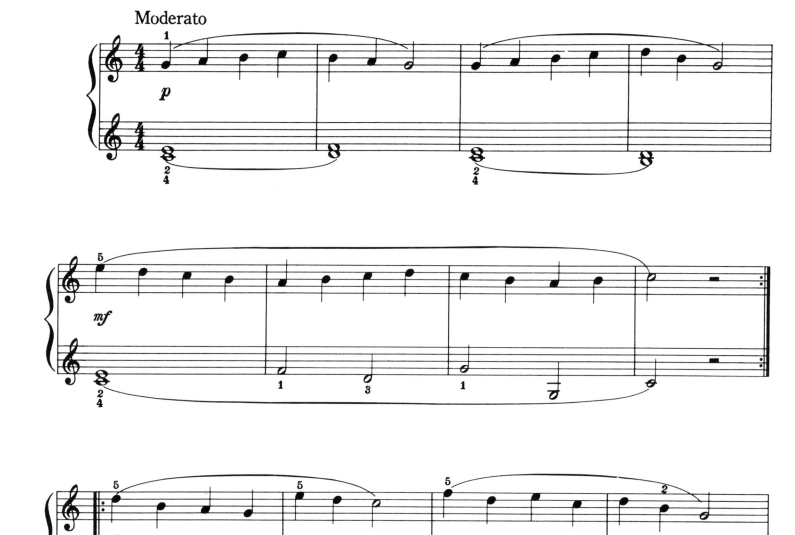

New World Symphony

Antonín Dvôrák

The Doll's Complaint

César Franck

113

Entry of the Gladiators

J. Fucik

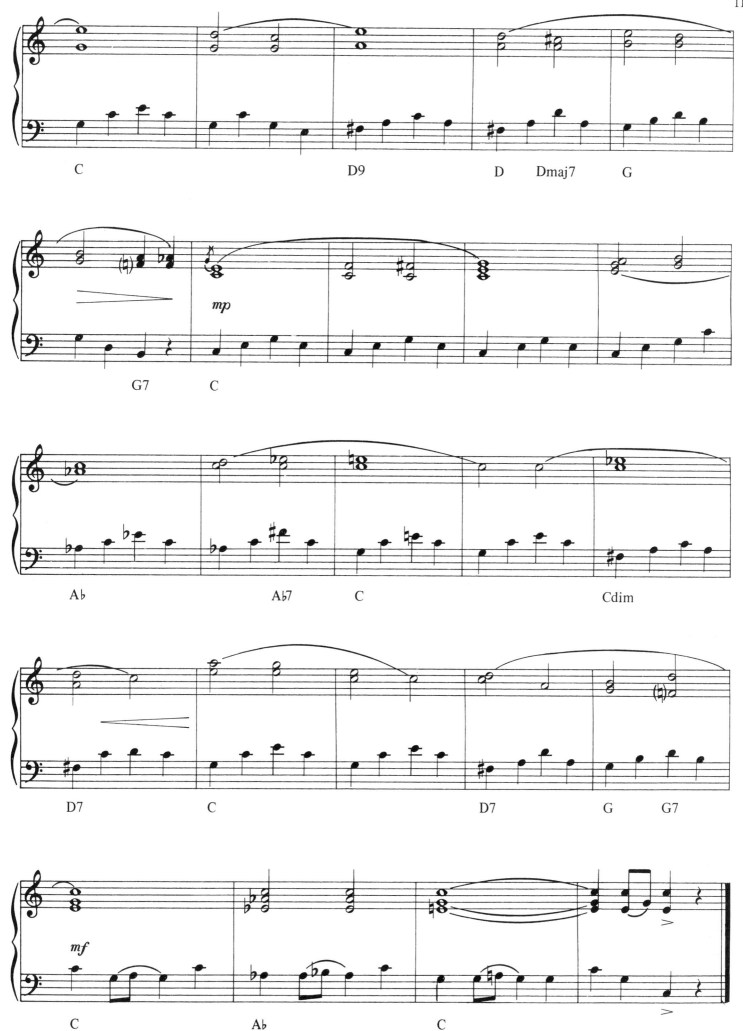

The Flowers That Bloom in the Spring

words by William Gilbert

music by Arthur Sullivan

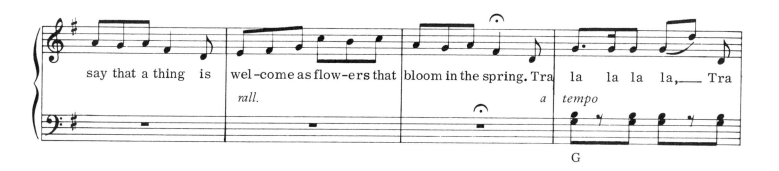
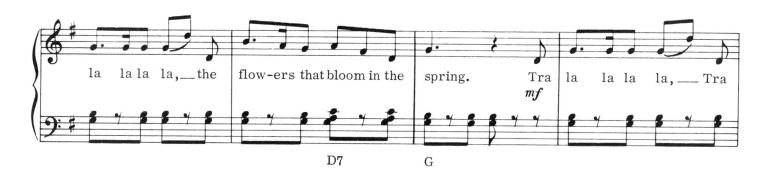

Little Buttercup

words by William Gilbert

music by Arthur Sullivan

(Mrs Cripps)

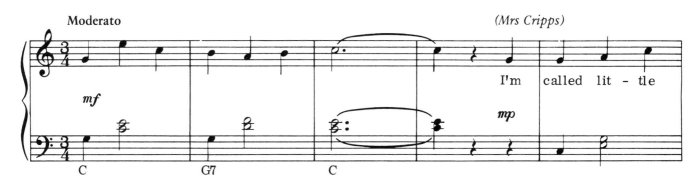

I'm called lit - tle

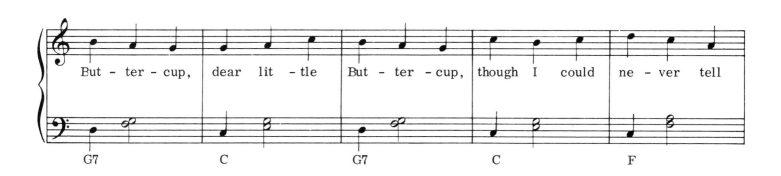

But - ter - cup, dear lit - tle But - ter - cup, though I could ne - ver tell

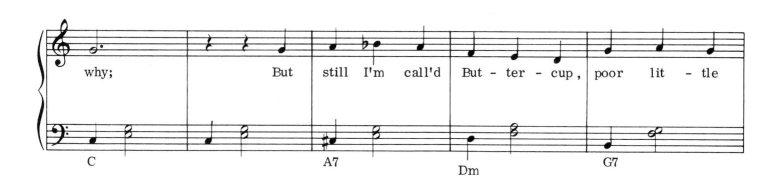

why; But still I'm call'd But - ter - cup, poor lit - tle

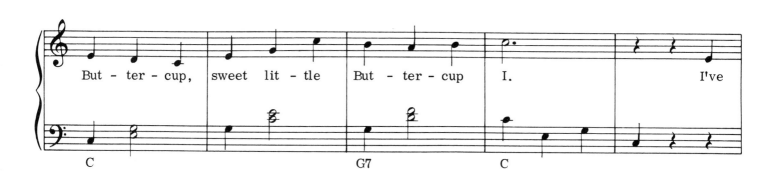

But - ter - cup, sweet lit - tle But - ter - cup I. I've

122

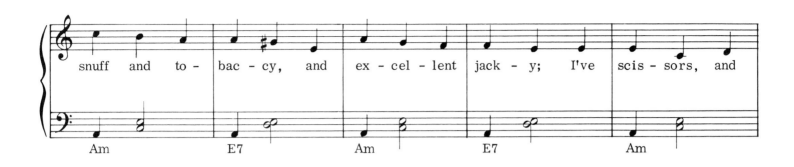

snuff and to - bac - cy, and ex - cel - lent jack - y; I've scis - sors, and

Am   E7   Am   E7   Am

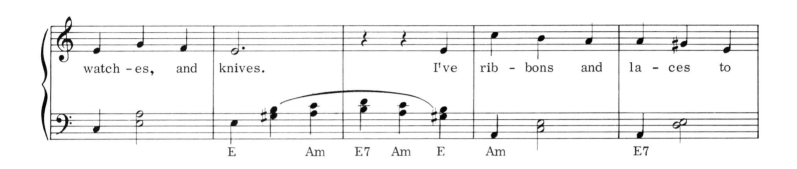

watch - es, and knives.   I've rib - bons and la - ces to

E   Am E7 Am E   Am   E7

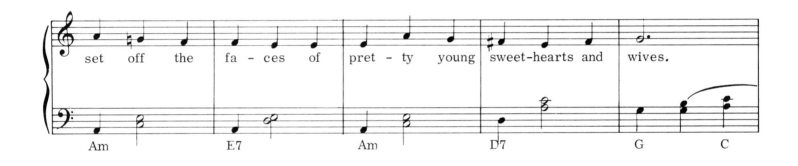

set off the fa - ces of pret - ty young sweet-hearts and wives.

Am   E7   Am   D7   G   C

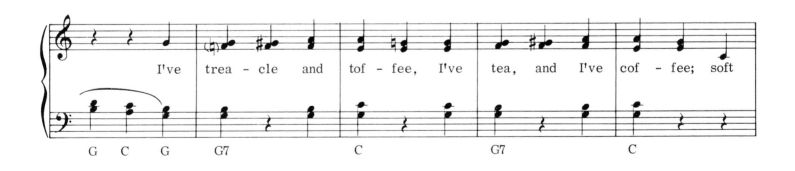

I've trea - cle and tof - fee, I've tea, and I've cof - fee; soft

G   C   G   G7   C   G7   C

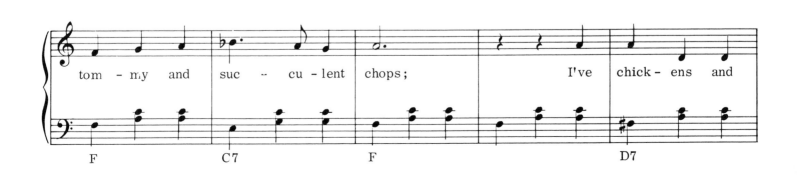

tom - my and suc - cu - lent chops;   I've chick - ens and

F   C7   F   D7

He Is an Englishman

words by William Gilbert

music by Arthur Sullivan

I Have a Song to Sing, O!

words by William Gilbert

music by Arthur Sullivan

To Coda ⊕

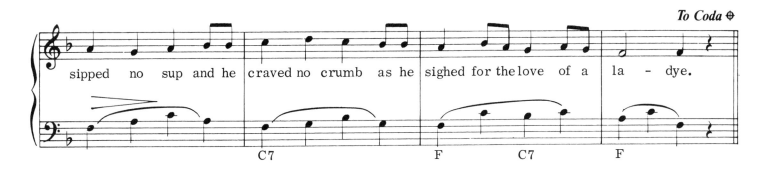

sipped no sup and he craved no crumb as he sighed for the love of a la - dye.

C7   F   C7   F

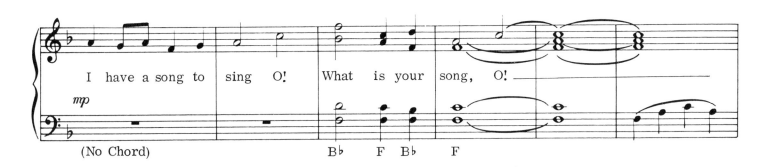

I have a song to sing O! What is your song, O! ____

mp

(No Chord)   B♭ F B♭ F

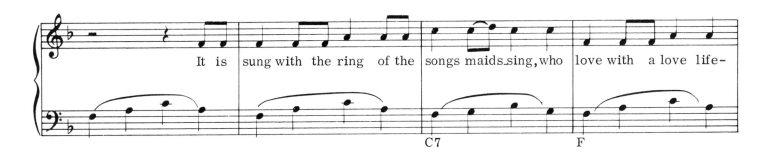

It is sung with the ring of the songs maids sing, who love with a love life-

C7   F

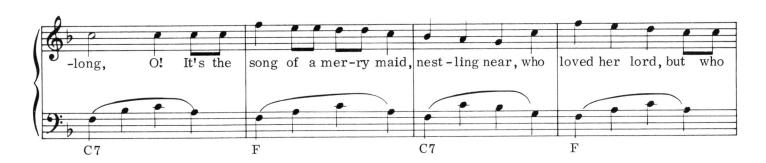

-long, O! It's the song of a mer-ry maid, nest-ling near, who loved her lord, but who

C7   F   C7   F

D. S. al Coda

⊕ *CODA*

dropped a tear at the

C7

mf

(No Chord)   F

Nothing Venture, Nothing Win

words by William Gilbert

music by Arthur Sullivan

130

Sing "Hey to You, Good-Day to You"

words by William Gilbert

music by Arthur Sullivan

132

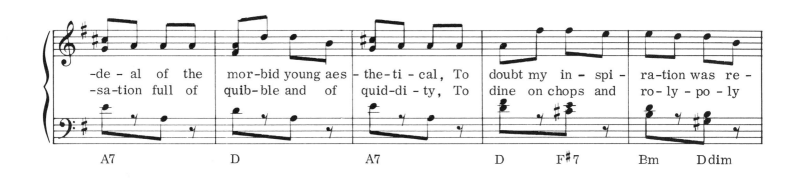

-de - al of the | mor-bid young aes - the-ti - cal, To | doubt my in - spi - | ration was re-
-sa-tion full of | quib-ble and of | quid-di - ty, To | dine on chops and | ro - ly - po - ly

A7 | D | A7 | D F#7 | Bm Ddim

-gard-ed as he- | re - ti-cal, Un- | til you cut me | out with your pla- | ci - di - ty e-
pud-ding with a- | vi - di-ty, He'd | bet-ter clear a- | way with all con- | ve - ni-ent ra-

A | D | F#7 | Bm Ddim | D A

-me-ti-cal." Sing | "Booh to you, Pooh | pooh to you" And | that's what I shall | say! Sing
-pi -di-ty." Sing | "Hey to you, Good | -day to you" And | that's what you should | say! Sing

D | | | Cm7 Fb7 | D7

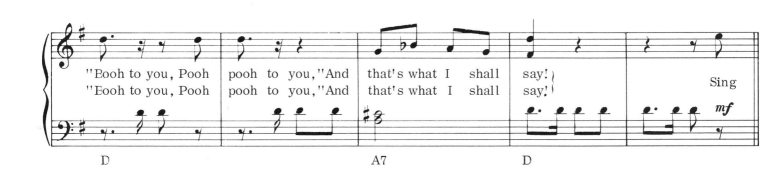

"Booh to you, Pooh | pooh to you," And | that's what I shall | say! }
"Booh to you, Pooh | pooh to you," And | that's what I shall | say! } | Sing

D | | A7 | D

"Hey to you, Good- | day to you" Sing | "Bah to you, Ha! | Ha! to you" Sing | "Booh to you, Pooh

G | | D9

Tit-Willow

words by William Gilbert

music by Arthur Sullivan

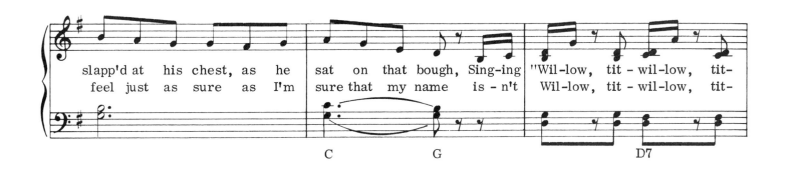

slapp'd at his chest, as he | sat on that bough, Sing-ing | "Wil-low, tit-wil-low, tit-
feel just as sure as I'm | sure that my name is-n't | Wil-low, tit-wil-low, tit-

C G D7

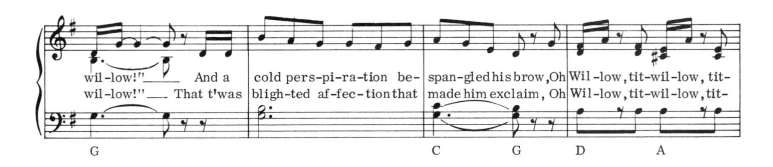

wil-low!"_____ And a | cold pers-pi-ra-tion be- | span-gled his brow,Oh | Wil-low,tit-wil-low, tit-
wil-low!"_____ That t'was | bligh-ted af-fec-tion that | made him exclaim, Oh | Wil-low,tit-wil-low, tit-

G C G D A

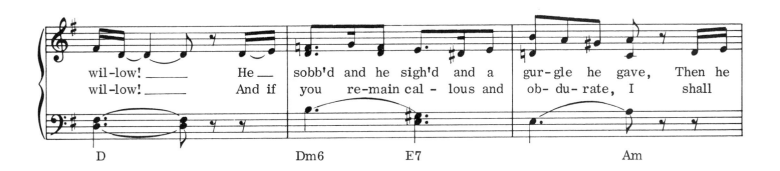

wil-low! _____ He __ | sobb'd and he sigh'd and a | gur-gle he gave, Then he
wil-low! _____ And if | you re-main cal-lous and | ob-du-rate, I shall

D Dm6 E7 Am

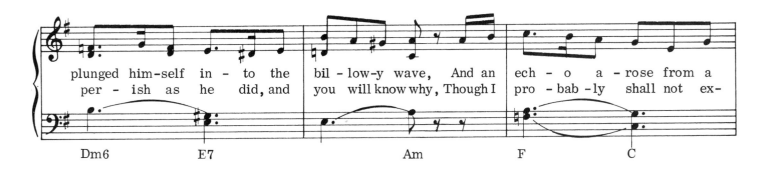

plunged him-self in - to the | bil - low-y wave, And an | ech - o a - rose from a
per - ish as he did, and | you will know why, Though I | pro - bab -ly shall not ex-

Dm6 E7 Am F C

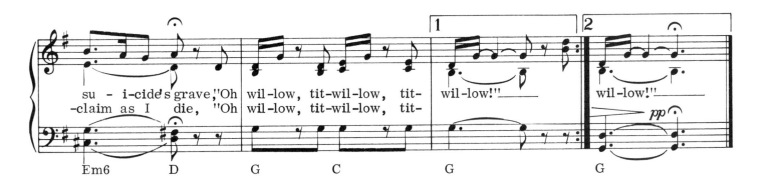

1 **2**
su - i-cide's grave,"Oh | wil-low, tit-wil-low, tit- | wil-low!"_____ | wil-low!"_____
-claim as I die, "Oh | wil-low, tit-wil-low, tit- | | pp

Em6 D G C G G

When Britain Really Ruled the Waves

words by William Gilbert

music by Arthur Sullivan

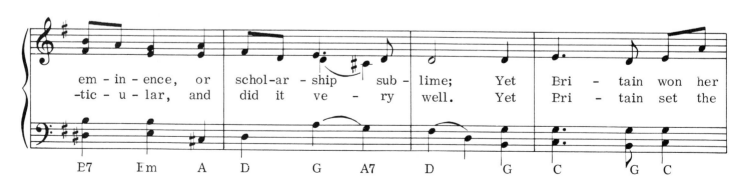

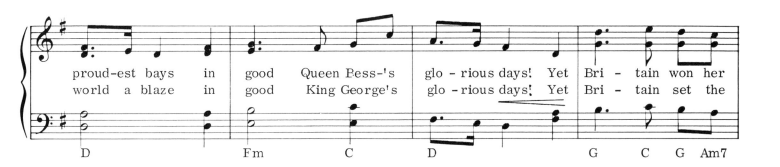

proud-est bays   in   good   Queen Bess-'s   glo - rious days! Yet   Bri - tain won her
world a blaze   in   good   King George's   glo - rious days! Yet   Bri - tain set the

D   Fm   C   D   G   C G Am7

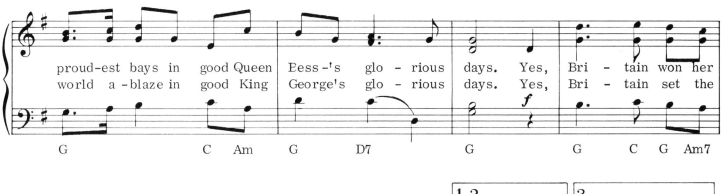

proud-est bays in   good Queen   Bess-'s   glo - rious   days.   Yes,   Bri - tain won her
world a -blaze in   good King   George's   glo - rious   days.   Yes,   Bri - tain set the

G   C Am   G   D7   G   G   C G Am7

1.2.   **3.**

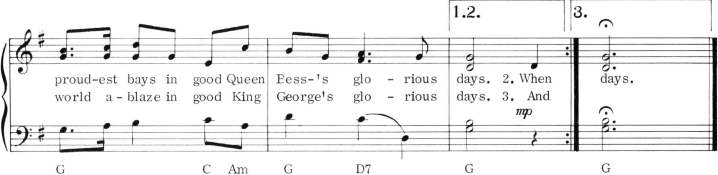

proud-est bays in   good Queen   Bess-'s   glo - rious   days. 2. When   days.
world a - blaze in   good King   George's   glo - rious   days. 3. And

G   C Am   G   D7   G   G

3. And while the House of Peers withholds
    Its legislative hand,
    And noble statesmen do not itch
    To interfere with matters which
    They do not understand;
    As bright will shine Great Britain's rays
    As in King George's glorious days!

Take a Pair of Sparkling Eyes

words by William Gilbert

music by Arthur Sullivan

139

Polka

Mikhail Ivanovich Glinka

March
from Alceste

Christoph Willibald Gluck

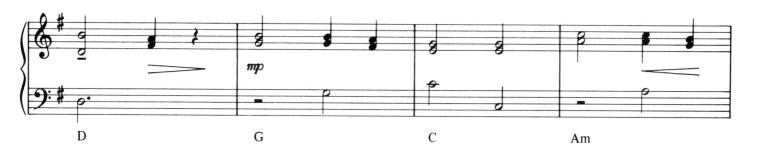

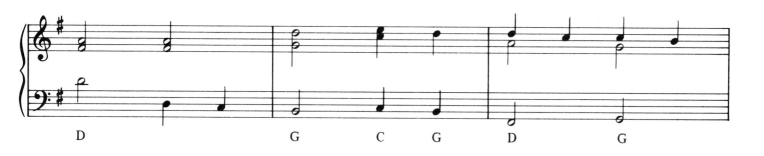

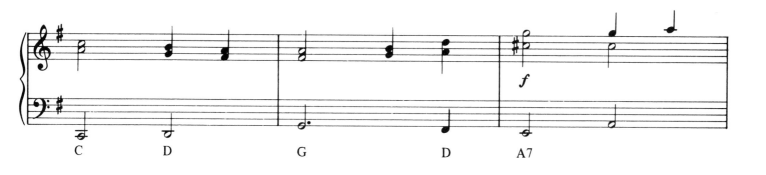

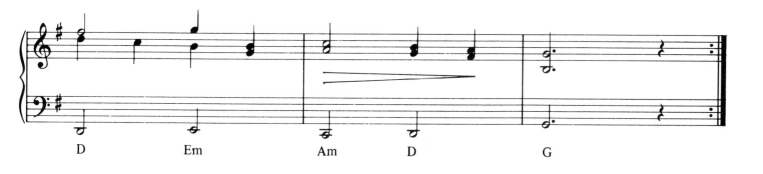

Morning

Edvard Grieg

145

Piano Concerto

Edvard Grieg

A Song

Cornelius Gurlitt

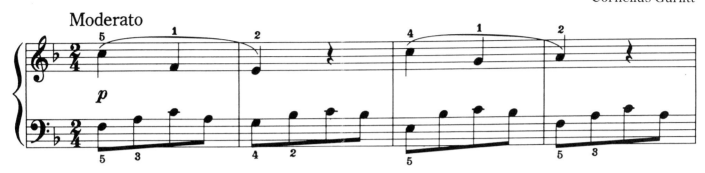

Air
from the Water Music

George Frideric Handel

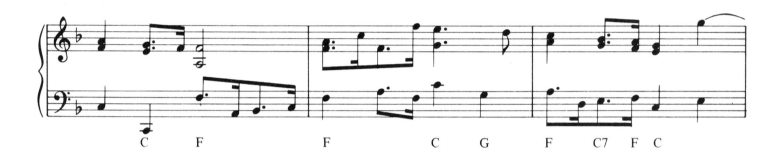

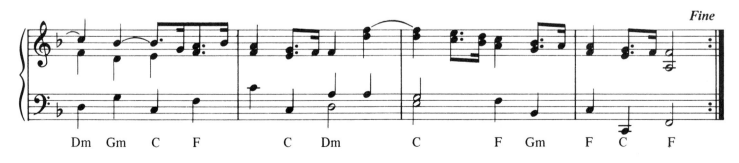

Bourrée
from Music for the Royal Fireworks

George Frideric Handel

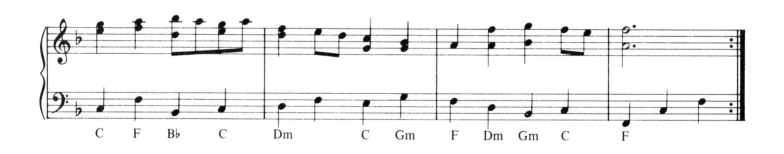

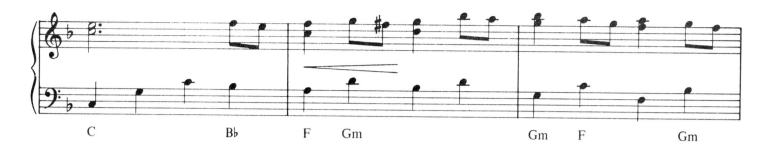

C   Bb   F   Gm   Gm   F   Gm

C   A7   Dm   A7   A   Dm   Gm   G   Am   A7

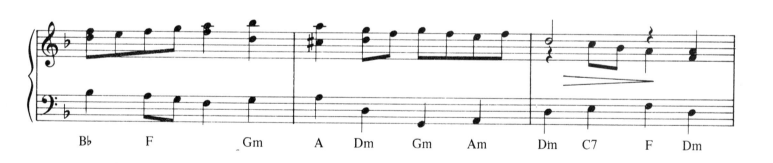

Bb   F   Gm   A   Dm   Gm   Am   Dm   C7   F   Dm

Gm   G   Am   A   Bb   Dm   F   Gm   A7   Dm   A   Dm

Gavotte

George Frideric Handel

Minuet No. 1
from Music for the Royal Fireworks

George Frideric Handel

Minuet No. 2
from Music for the Royal Fireworks

George Frideric Handel

Theme
from 2nd Movement Symphony No. 101 (The Clock)

Franz Joseph Haydn

155

German Dance

Franz Joseph Haydn

157

Trio

D. C. al Fine

The Chrysanthemum

Scott Joplin

160

The Entertainer

Scott Joplin

The Easy Winners

Scott Joplin

Eugenia

Scott Joplin

169

Heliotrope Bonquet

Scott Joplin and Louis Chauvin

Maple Leaf Rag

Scott Joplin

Ragtime Dance

Scott Joplin

The Strenuous Life

Scott Joplin

187

189

The Sycamore

Scott Joplin

Bourrée

Johann Krieger

Four Scottish Dances

Friedrich Kuhlau

II

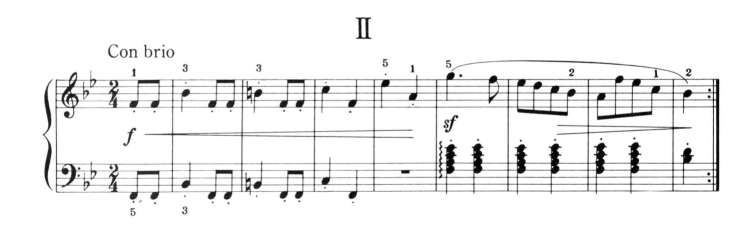

III

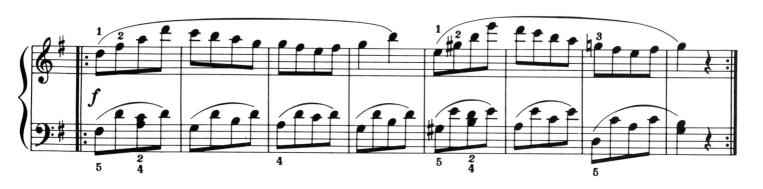

IV

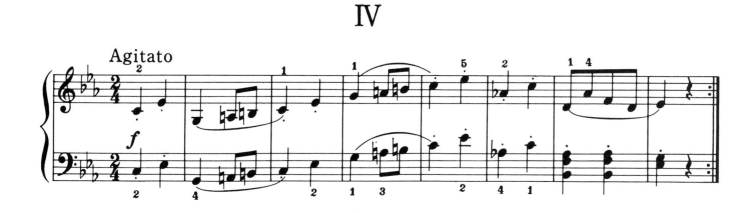

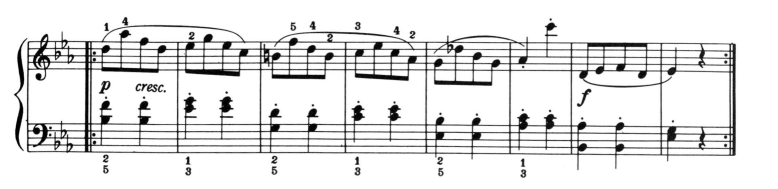

Liebestraum

Franz Liszt

To a Wild Rose

Edward MacDowell

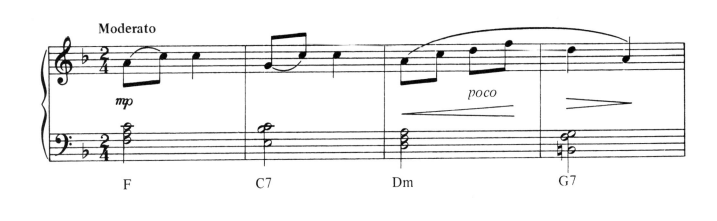

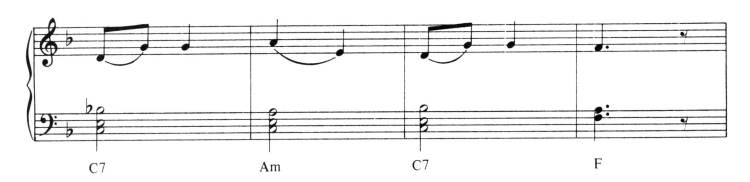

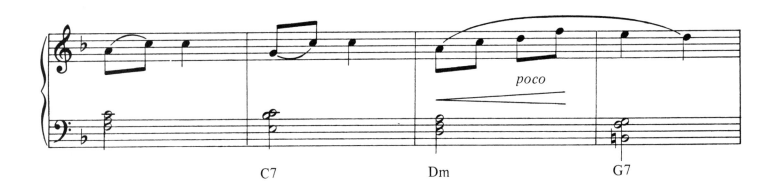

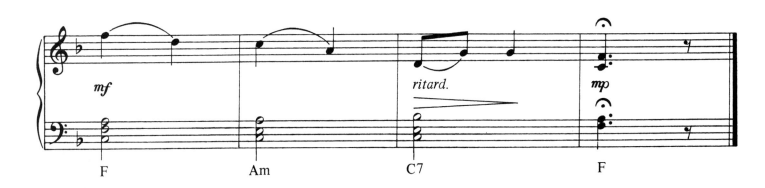

Fingal's Cave

Felix Mendelssohn

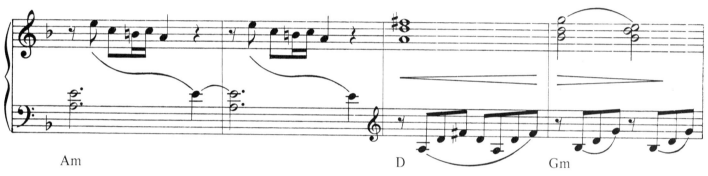

Nocturne
from A Midsummer Night's Dream

Felix Mendelssohn

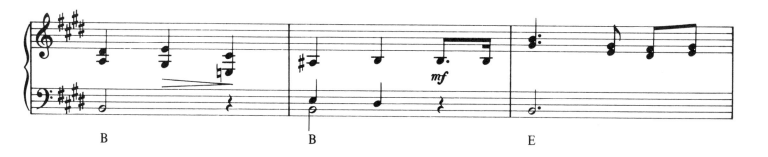

B   B   E

B7   B7   A   B

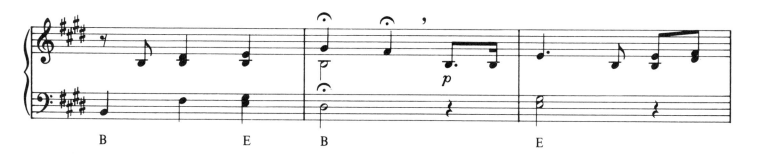

B   E   B   E

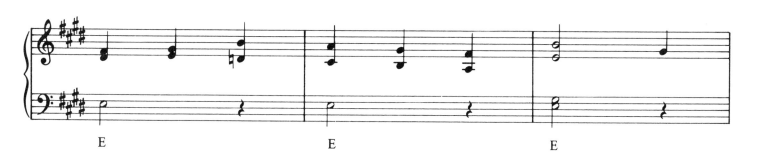

E   E   E

F#7   B   F#m   B7   E

Spring Song

Felix Mendelssohn

Wedding Marches

Felix Mendelssohn/Richard Wagner

Wedding March – Mendelssohn

Two Minuets
from the Notebook for Nannerl

Leopold Mozart

Allegretto

II.

Andante

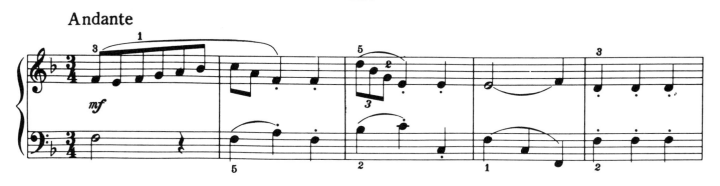

Eine Kleine Nachtmusik (Romance)

Wolfgang Amadeus Mozart

Andante

Eine Kleine Nachtmusik (Rondo)

Wolfgang Amadeus Mozart

Minuet In F, K. 2

Wolfgang Amadeus Mozart

Eine Kleine Nachtmusik (Serenade)

Wolfgang Amadeus Mozart

215

216

Minuet, K. 94

Wolfgang Amadeus Mozart

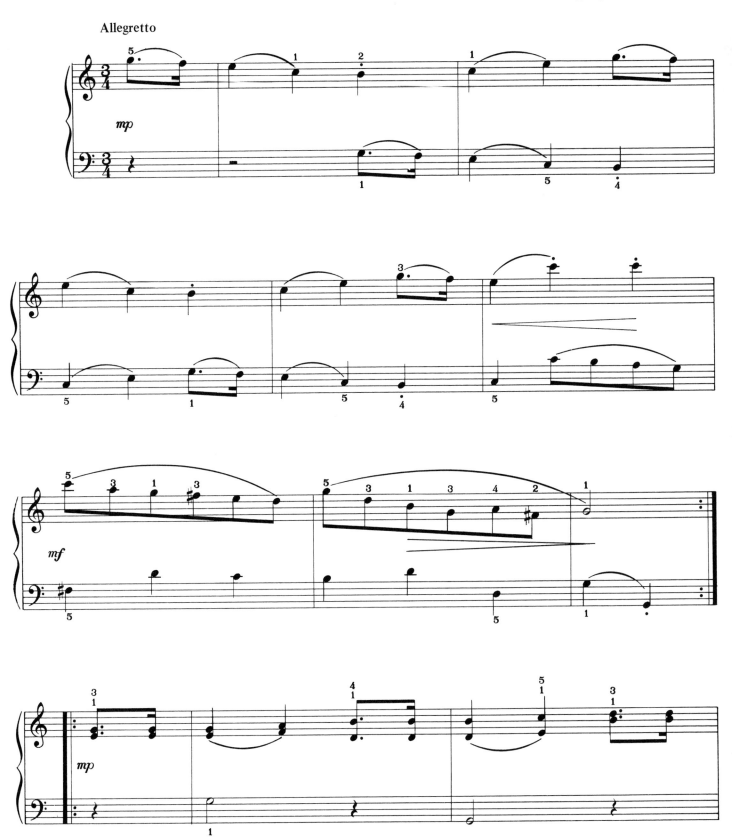

Rondo Alla Turca

Wolfgang Amadeus Mozart

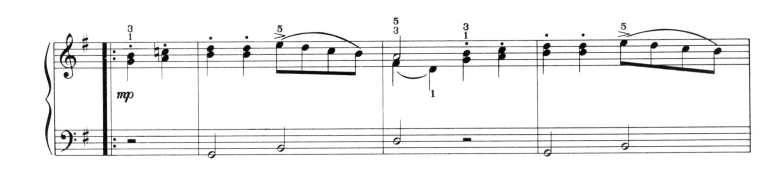

Romance from Piano Concerto No. 20
in D Minor, K. 466

Wolfgang Amadeus Mozart

Theme from Variations in A, K. 137

Wolfgang Amadeus Mozart

Theme from Piano Sonata in C

Wolfgang Amadeus Mozart

Theme from Symphony No. 40

Wolfgang Amadeus Mozart

Theme from a Musical Joke

Wolfgang Amadeus Mozart

The Cuckoo

August Eberhard Müller

Barcarolle
from Tales of Hoffman

Jacques Offenbach

236

237

One Fine Day
from Madame Butterfly

Giacomo Puccini

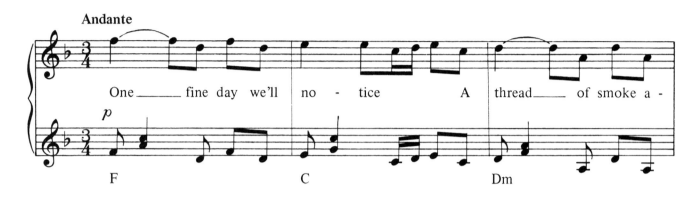

Poco meno mosso

climb - ing the hill - ock. Can you guess who it

* B   Em

più lento

is? and when he's reach'd the summit, can you guess what he'll say? He will call "Butter- fly," from the

G6   C

molto rall.

dis - tance. I, with-out ans - w'ring, hold my-self qui - et - ly con - ceal'd;___ a bit to

Dm6   C   Dm6   C

a tempo primo

tease him___ and a bit so as not to *ff* die___ at our first

Ped   F

rit.

meet - ing,_____ and thou a lit - tle trou-bled, he will call, he will call,___ "Dear

C   Dm   C

Musetta's Song
from La Bohème

Giacomo Puccini

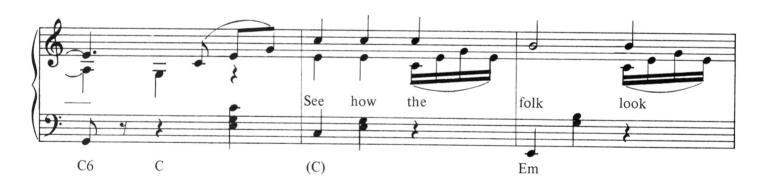

244

Minuet

Henry Purcell

Rondeau
from The Fairy Queen

Henry Purcell

Sailor's Dance

from Dido and Aeneas

Henry Purcell

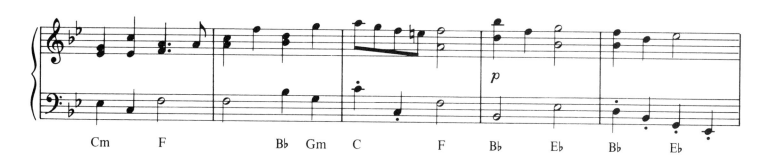

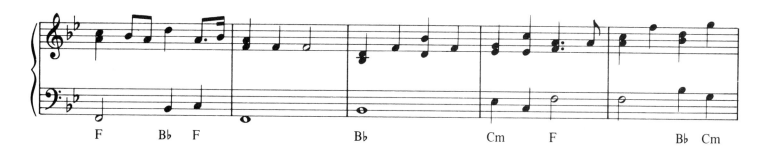

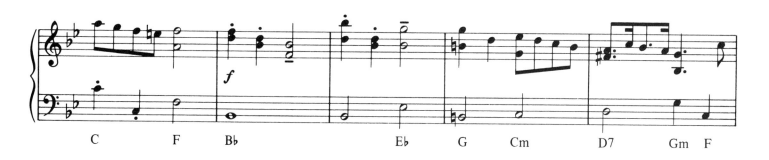

When I Am Laid in Earth

from Dido and Aeneas

Henry Purcell

Grave e largo

Melody in F

Anton Rubinstein

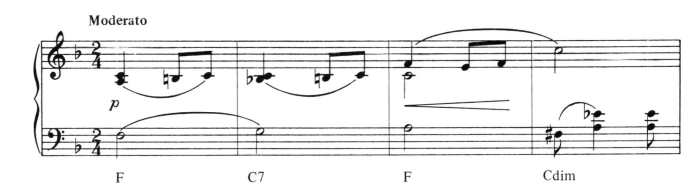

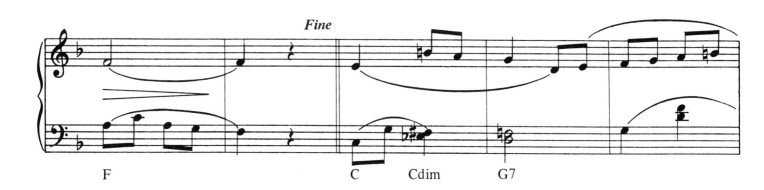

Softly Awakes My Heart

from Samson and Delilah

Camille Saint-Saëns

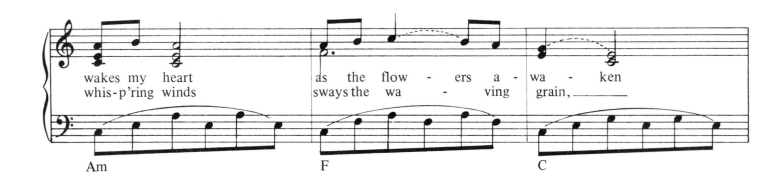

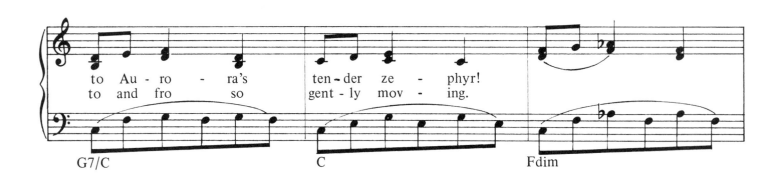

254

Sonata (Minuet)

Domenico Scarlatti

Ave Maria

Franz Schubert

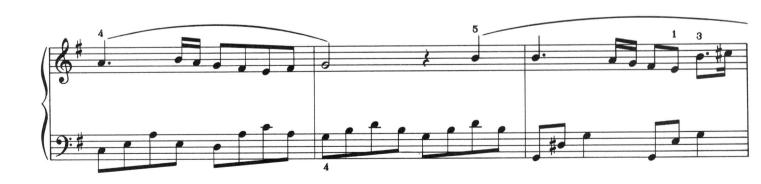

257

Death and the Maiden

Franz Schubert

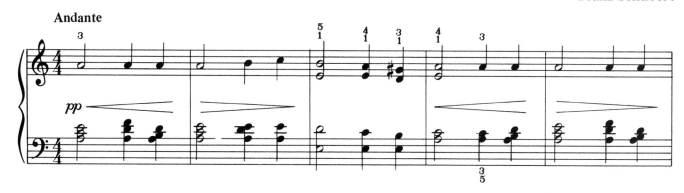

Ballet Music from Rosamunde

Franz Schubert

Impromptu Op. 90, No. 1

Franz Schubert

Moderato

Moment Musical Op. 94, No. 3

Franz Schubert

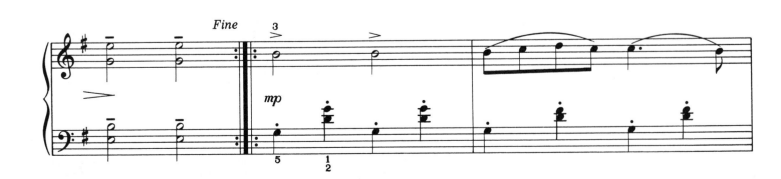

Marche Militaire

Franz Schubert

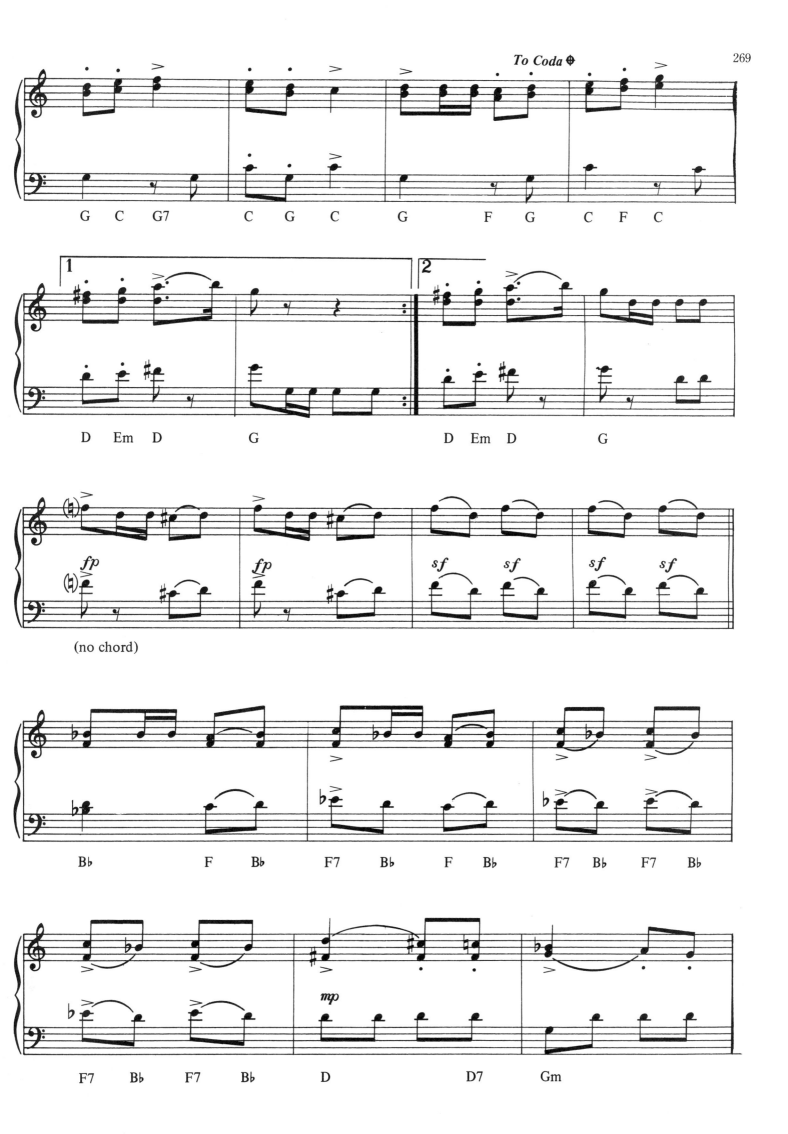

Piano Trio in E Flat (Slow Movement)

Franz Schubert

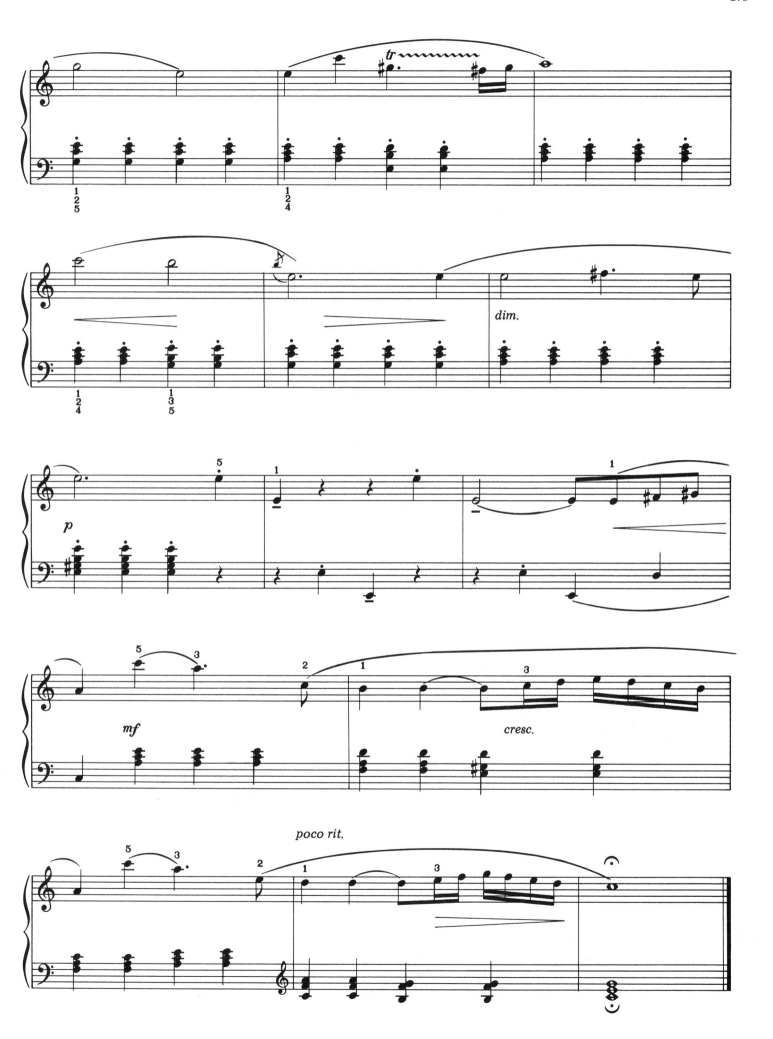

Serenade

Franz Schubert

Symphony in B Flat (2nd Movement)

Franz Schubert

The Trout

Franz Schubert

Moderato

Unfinished Symphony (Theme)

Franz Schubert

Allegro moderato

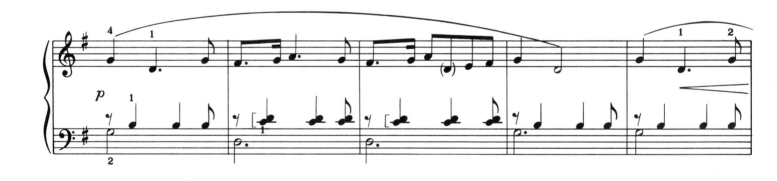

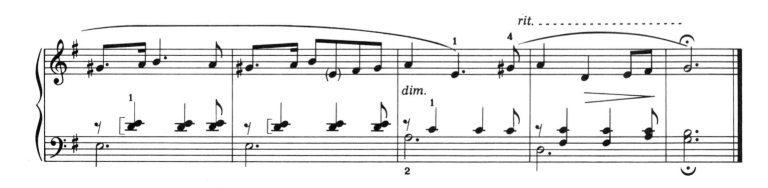

Chorale

Robert Schumann

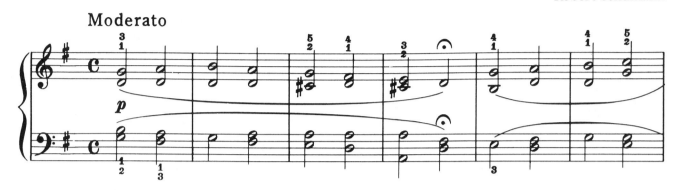

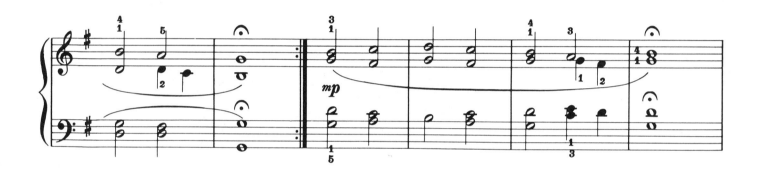

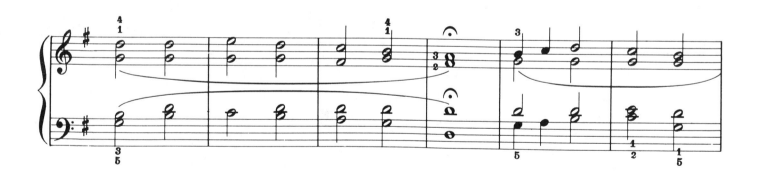

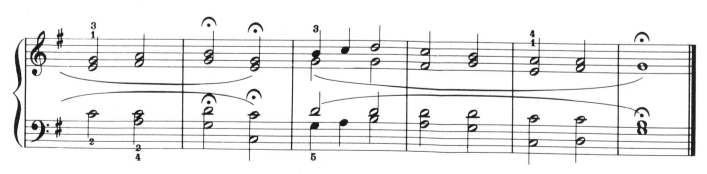

Dreaming

Robert Schumann

Slumber Song

Robert Schumann

285

The Happy Farmer

Robert Schumann

Vltava

Bedrich Smetana

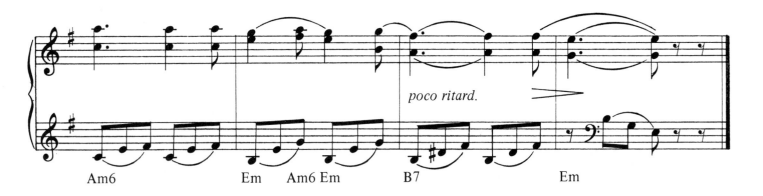

The Stars and Stripes Forever

John Philip Sousa

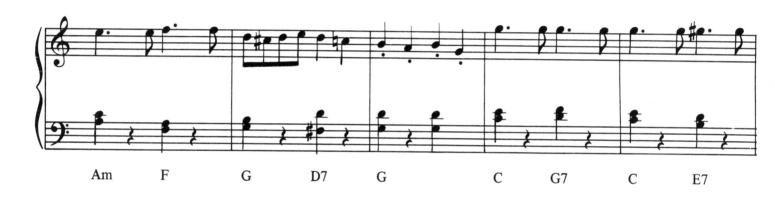

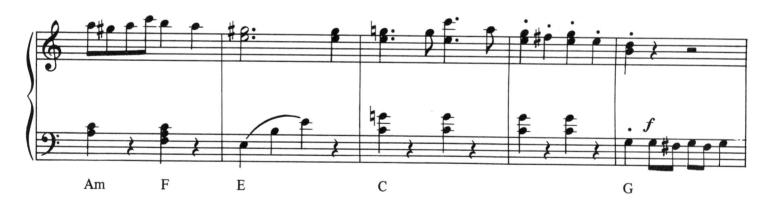

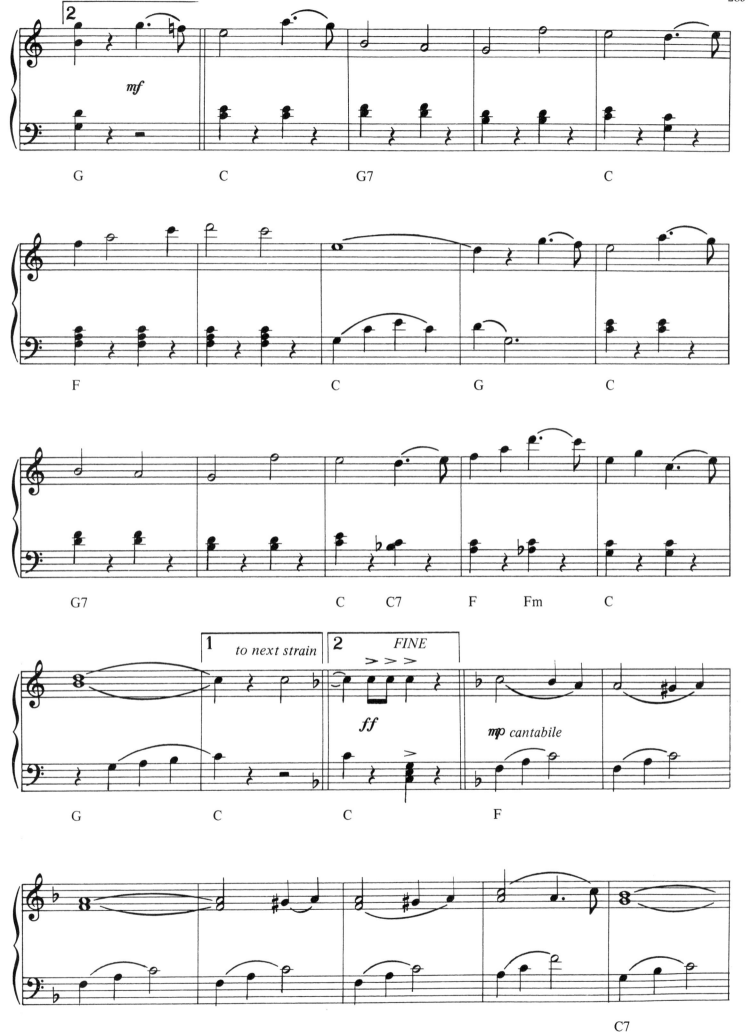

290

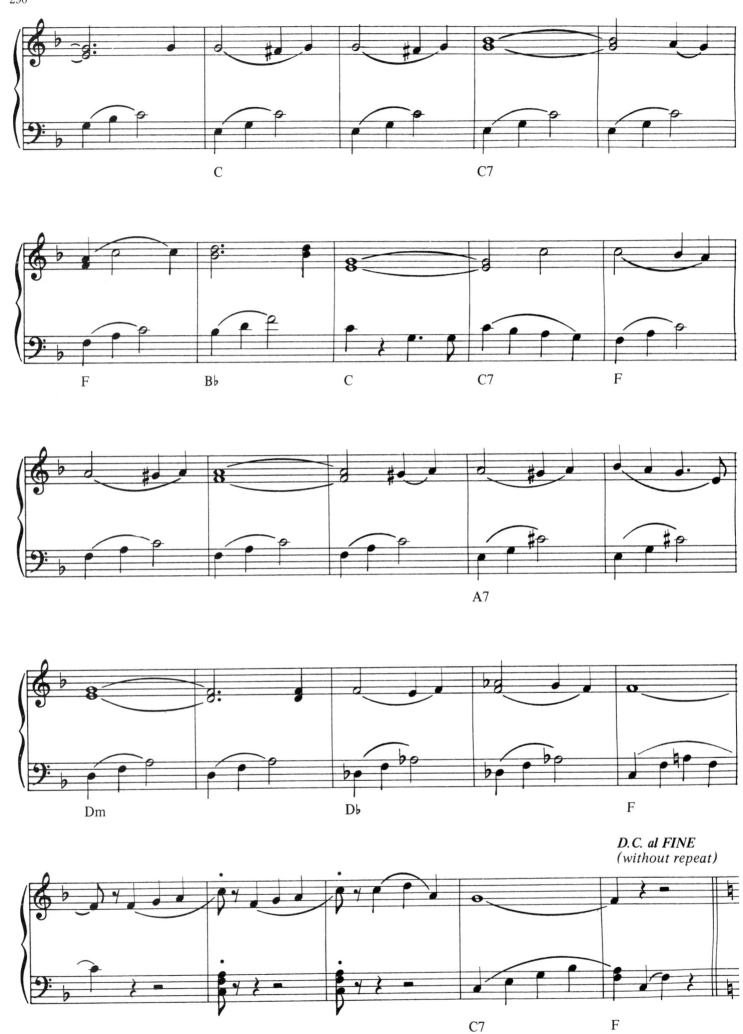

Washington Post

John Philip Sousa

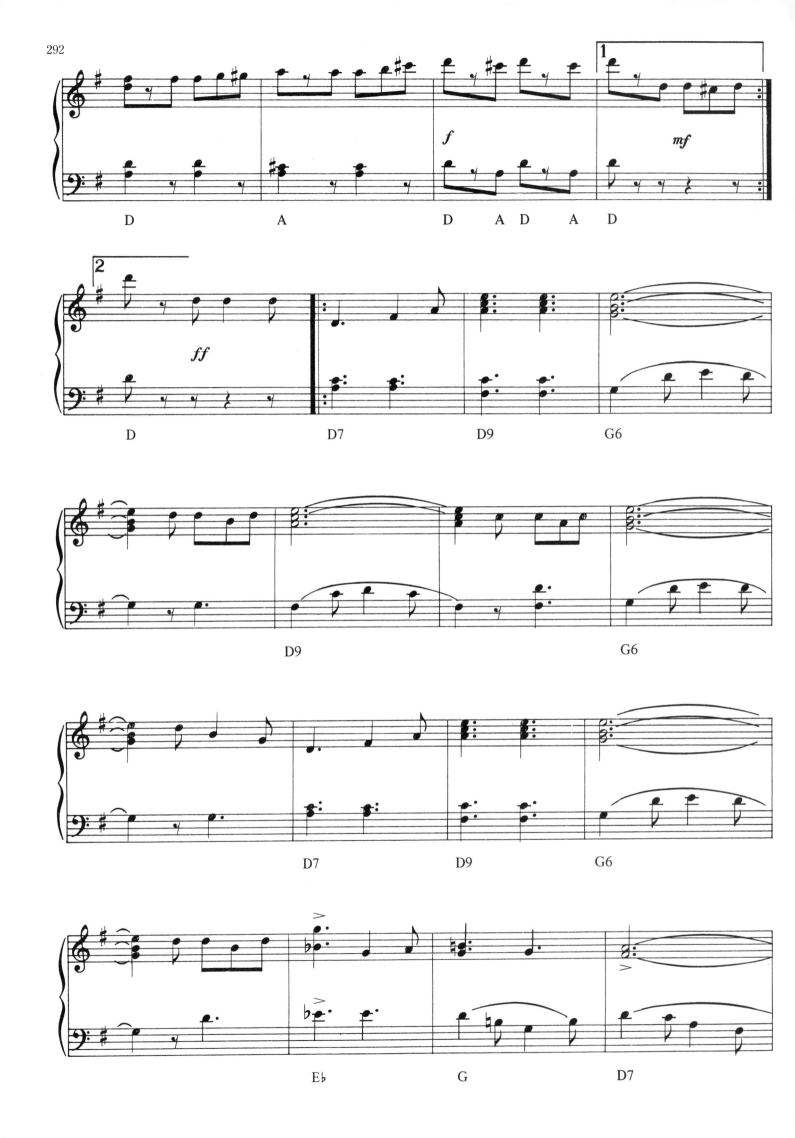

The Beautiful Blue Danube Op. 314

Johann Strauss, Jr.

Die Fledermaus (Overture) Op. 362

Johann Strauss, Jr.

301

Emperor Waltz Op. 437

Johann Strauss, Jr.

The Laughing Song

from Die Fledermaus

Johann Strauss, Jr.

A __ man like you, a __ Mar - quis too you real __ ly
This straight pro - file in __ gre - cian style all scru - ples

should __ be - ware. _____ I __ should ad - vise,
should __ dis - arm. _____ If you still should doubt,

308

Pizzicato Polka

Johann Strauss, Jr. and Josef Strauss

D

Coda

Radetzky March

Johann Strauss, Jr.

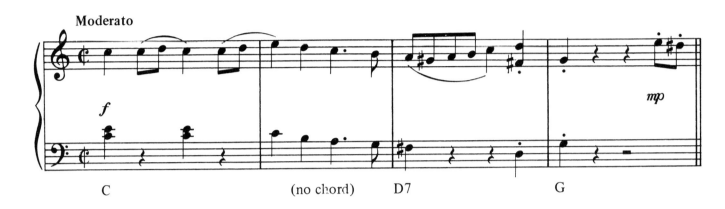

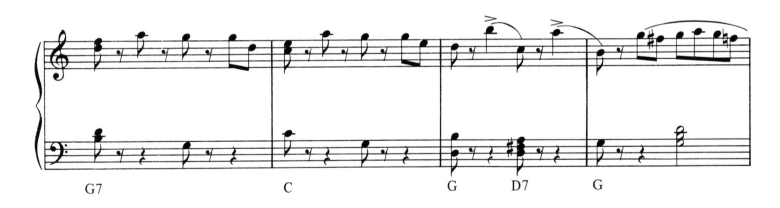

Tales from the Vienna Woods Op. 388

Johann Strauss, Jr.

Tritsch Tratsch Polka Op. 214

Johann Strauss, Jr.

Tempo di Polka

You and You
from Die Fledermaus

Johann Strauss, Jr.

Little Fairy Waltz

Ludovic Streabbog

325

Dance of the Sugar Plum Fairy

from Casse Noisette

Peter Ilyich Tchaikovsky

Sleeping Beauty Waltz

Peter Ilyich Tchaikovsky

Moderately with expression

332

333

334

Swan Lake Waltz

from Swan Lake

Peter Ilyich Tchaikovsky

Symphony Pathétique

Peter Ilyich Tchaikovsky

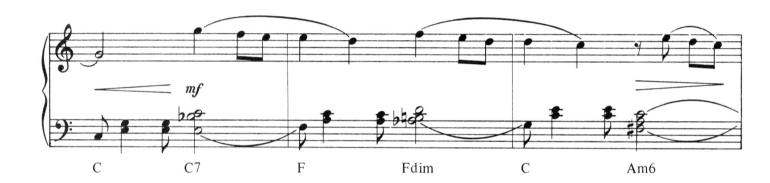

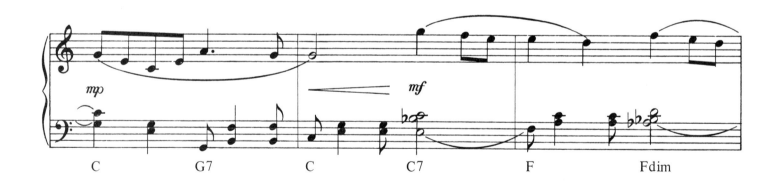

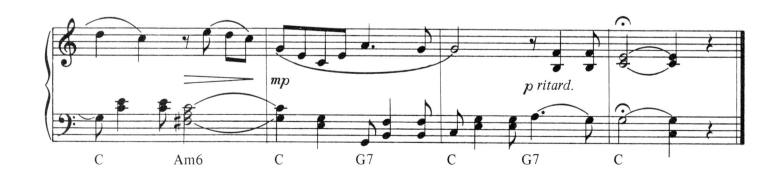

Valse des fleurs

from Casse Noisette

Peter Ilyich Tchaikovsky

342

Under the Double Eagle

J.F. Wagner

Anvil Chorus
from Il Trovatore

Giuseppe Verdi

Pilgrims' Chorus
from Tannhäuser

Richard Wagner

The Evening Star
from Tannhäuser

Richard Wagner